# Pets and Their Famous Humans

PRESTEL

MUNICH · LONDON · NEW YORK

# LIST
### OF
# PETS AND THEIR FAMOUS HUMANS

### 01
# Granizo
FRIDA KAHLO'S
FAWN
Page 4

### 02
# Archie
ANDY WARHOL'S
FRIEND FOR LIFE
Page 6

### 03
# Katze
GUSTAV KLIMT'S
FURRY COMPANION
Page 8

### 04
# Pinka
VIRGINIA WOOLF'S
INSPIRATION
Page 10

### 05
# Grip
CHARLES DICKENS'S
TALKING RAVEN
Page 12

### 06
# Crocodiles in the Bathtub
DOROTHY PARKER'S CROCODILES
Page 14

### 07
# Babou
SALVADOR DALÍ'S
PAINTED CAT
Page 16

### 08
# Bibo
ALBERT EINSTEIN'S
SAD PARROT
Page 18

### 09
# Jofi
SIGMUND FREUD'S
HELPER
Page 20

### 10
# Diamond
ISAAC NEWTON'S
CLUMSY CHUM
Page 22

### 11
# Lump
PABLO PICASSO'S
DARLING
Page 24

### 12
# Starling
WOLFGANG AMADEUS MOZART'S
FEATHERED IMITATOR
Page 26

### 13
# Snowball
ERNEST HEMINGWAY'S
LUCKY CAT
Page 28

### 14
# Bustopher Jones, Mungojerrie & Rumpleteazer
T.S. ELIOT'S CATS
Page 30

### 15
# Puce
HENRI MATISSE'S
BLACK CAT
Page 32

### 16
# Pluto & Elia
LUCIAN FREUD'S
MODELS
Page 34

### 17
# Choupette
KARL LAGERFELD'S
MEDIA STAR
Page 36

### 18
# Stanley & Boodgie
DAVID HOCKNEY'S
DACHSHUNDS
Page 38

### 19
# Bo & Chia
GEORGIA O'KEEFFE'S
CHOW CHOWS
Page 40

### 20
# Bimbo
PAUL KLEE'S
WHITE TOMCAT
Page 42

# Granizo

FRIDA KAHLO'S FAWN ⊰

Frida Kahlo was born in Casa Azul, also known as the Blue House, in a suburb of Mexico City. She spent most of her life there. When she was eighteen, she was in a terrible bus accident that left her bedridden for many months. That was when she began painting.

Because it was difficult for Frida to travel outside her home, the courtyard of the Blue House became her little universe. Together with her husband, Diego Rivera, also a famous artist, she transformed the courtyard into a marvelous forest for her many exotic pet animals. In the center of the courtyard was a small Aztec pyramid built by Diego. The couple's pet osprey was usually perched on top. Because the bird pooped on everything, they named it Gertrudis Caca Blanca, which means Gertrude Whitepoop!

Frida Kahlo loved her animals very much and allowed them to roam freely about the house. She had spider monkeys, parrots, hens, and Mexican hairless dogs, of which Mr. Xoloti was her favorite. Granizo was a sweet fawn she raised in the house. Even when it eventually grew antlers, it nestled up to Frida in her bed.

The animals were more than companions and playmates. Like herself, they often appeared in her paintings. Granizo can be seen in two of Frida's most important works. In the larger of the two, *The Wounded Table* (1940), it is still a little fawn with white spots. Six years later, its fully grown body can be seen in the famous picture, *The Wounded Deer*. This painting shows how Frida felt when she learned that she would never fully heal from her accident. In many ways, Frida's paintings and her pets helped her to live with her lifelong pain.

### Frida Kahlo (1907-1954)

The Mexican painter was not only famous for her art, but also for the way she lived, wore her hair, and how she dressed. In her self-portraits, she painted herself just as she was, with big, bushy eyebrows and a body full of scars from the many operations following her accident. Casa Azul is now an art museum and her paintings have been declared a national cultural heritage by the Mexican government.

# Archie

## ✦ ANDY WARHOL'S FRIEND FOR LIFE ✦

Andy Warhol never saw himself owning a dog. He had lived only with cats as a child, all of whom were named Sam. Then on Christmas day in 1973, a dark, short-haired dachshund named Archie entered his life. The two became lifelong friends. Andy was already a world-famous artist by then, best known for painting objects like soup cans and Coca Cola bottles, things familiar to everyone through advertising and everyday life. It was a completely new way of painting called "Pop Art."

Wherever Andy went, he always arrived with little Archie in his arms. At fancy restaurants, Andy would cover Archie with a napkin so no one could spot him sitting on his lap. If he did not feel like answering a question in an interview, he would turn to Archie and say, "You say something, Archie!" The dog, however, would simply turn up his nose. On the other hand, Archie seemed to like posing in front of flashing cameras, as if to show off the gold charm from Tiffany & Co. dangling from his collar.

In 1976, Andy Warhol found a playmate for Archie, a light-brown dachshund named Amos. Amos didn't like being around people as much as Archie did. This led to Archie giving up the limelight to romp around with Amos. That same year, Andy immortalized Archie in the painting *Dachshund (Archie)*. The two dogs remained his faithful chums right up to his death in 1987.

### Andy Warhol (1928-1987)

Andy Warhol's real name was Andrew Warhola. The son of Slovakian immigrants started out working as a commercial artist and illustrator before he began creating his own work in the 1960s. From 1962, he worked in a studio called the Factory in downtown New York, where he also made films. Many of his works were a series of the same image made in different colors. His love of animals can be seen in the series of pictures called *Endangered Species*.

# Katze

✛ GUSTAV KLIMT'S FURRY COMPANION ✛

From an early age, the Austrian painter Gustav Klimt showed a keen artistic talent. Later, while studying in an arts and crafts school, Gustav and his brother ran a successful workshop painting murals and ceilings inside large, famous buildings. In 1888, Gustav received a Golden Order of Merit from Emperor Franz Joseph I for the murals he painted inside the Burgtheater of Vienna.

After his brother's death, Klimt preferred to work on his own in a light-filled studio where he could let his creativity run wild. His studio was in the center of Vienna, surrounded by a large garden. It was the perfect place to work outside the "art rules" of the time. For similar reasons, Gustav took off his clothes when he entered the studio and wore only a light, flowing tunic when he painted. His mosaic-like images were populated with plants, geometric patterns, and sweeping lines—a style that had never been seen before.

In addition to famous artists of the time, Gustav's studio and garden also swarmed with cats. They climbed the trees, traipsed among the canvases, leapt onto the laps of the women who were sitting as models for the artist, and played with the many sketches scattered about the floor. One of the few photos of Gustav shows him in his tunic, cradling one of the cats. The cats also performed an important task. When visitors passed by the studio, they were struck by the strong smell of urine. Gustav used this as a varnish to preserve his sketches. He was especially fond of a black-and-white spotted feline he simply called Katze. Katze accompanied him for many years and was at his side during the creation of important works like *The Kiss* (1908), which brought him great success during his lifetime.

### Gustav Klimt (1862-1918)
One of the most famous artists to emerge from the Art Nouveau period, Gustav Klimt was renowned for his golden paintings. His work is recognized for the decorative way in which people and objects were painted. Plants, flowers, or ornate lines adorn Gustav Klimt's portraits and landscape paintings. At the beginning of the twentieth century, it was not only paintings that were created in this style, but also furniture and other everyday objects.

# Pinka

## ➤ VIRGINIA WOOLF'S INSPIRATION ➤

As a small child, Virginia Woolf discovered that there were two things in life that made her happy: writing and dogs. Her childhood companions were Shag, Jerry, and Gurth. As an adult, she first got a boxer dog from a pet sanctuary, then a terrier mix called Grizzle, and in 1926, at the age of forty-four, the very posh Pinka entered her life. This pedigree cocker spaniel was a gift from a fellow author, Vita Sackville-West.

Virginia did not want her pedigree Pinka to be as snooty as some of the aristocrats in London, so Pinka was allowed to lead a normal dog's life, which included running through fields, rolling in mud, and splashing in rivers.

Throughout her life, Virginia suffered periods of heavy sadness. On such days, she would spend the day in bed. It calmed her to feel Pinka at her side, especially when the two took long walks together, even if it was cold and rainy. Walking helped Virginia recover and gave her ideas for her work. While out strolling with Pinka, she used to recite whole paragraphs of her new books and then type them up when she got home.

Pinka played a big part in one of her books. Virginia decided to write a biography of the poet Elizabeth Barret Browning as if it were written by the poet's cocker spaniel, Flush. Virginia used Pinka as a role model since she knew nothing about Barret's dog. In the end, there was so much of Pinka's personality in Flush that a photo of Pinka was used on the book's cover. Though *Flush: A Biography* (1933) was not as serious as Woolf's other books, to everyone's surprise it was a great success. Two years later in 1935, Pinka suddenly died. Virginia didn't just miss Pinka's companionship and affection, she also missed her as an inspiration for her writing. In her journal, Virginia noted that a part of her had been buried along with Pinka at her cottage, Monk's House. In 1941, the author's own ashes were buried there.

### Virginia Woolf (1882-1941)

Adeline Virginia Stephen Woolf was born in London in 1882 and became interested in literature by spending time in her father's big library. Her novels are known around the world and translated into many languages. She also worked as a publisher and social critic. Today, she is seen as one of the most influential thinkers of the women's movement, which fights for equality between men and women.

# Grip

It's really no wonder that the English novelist Charles Dickens had an exceptional pet. After all, he did invent exceptional characters such as Oliver Twist. Grip the raven came to Charles through a friend who had found him in a park. Charles took him in and raised him. He taught Grip to communicate using gestures, sounds, and words. In return, he learned how to understand the language of birds. When Grip flapped his wings and cawed, it meant that he was happy. Then he would move toward his master's feet in little hops and open his beak to be fed.

Edgar Allen Poe, a fellow writer, was so fascinated by the bird that he was inspired to write one of his most famous works, the poem "The Raven."

Charles's family loved Grip very much, even though he constantly pecked them in the ankles for fun. His sons pleaded with their father to put the raven in one of his novels. So Charles came up with a fitting character for the novel *Barnaby Rudge* (1941), about a young simpleton who would be completely lost without his clever raven. If you read the novel, you can well imagine what the real Grip was like. How he would rock up and down, how he sat on the arm of a chair, how he would announce something with his croaky voice, or the way he would settle on the hand of the author, "as elegantly as a rider gets on to his horse."

Charles once said he did not know if this animal was a bird or a little devil. As an example, when Grip bit Topping the coachman, he had to go to the barn as a punishment, where he slept on the back of a horse. Grip also died there, having drunk from a paint bucket a few days earlier while the house was being painted. Before he keeled over, he let out one of his favorite expressions: "Hallo, old girl!"

### Charles Dickens (1812-1870)

No other writer described the social ills of the England of his age as impressively as Charles Dickens. Born in Landport near Portsmouth, Charles had to support his family from a young age. He worked as a legal assistant until he published his first novel in 1836, followed by many more. By the way, Grip is now a literary memorial. The stuffed raven can be found in the Free Library in Philadelphia, Pennsylvania, USA.

# Crocodiles in the Bathtub

## ✦ DOROTHY PARKER'S CROCODILES ✦

After finishing her basic education, Dorothy Parker had to take up work immediately and make her own way in life. College was not in her future. Her mother died when she was quite small and her father did not live long enough to see her twentieth birthday. Despite her background, Dorothy read and wrote as much as she could. Eventually she became a famous critic of New York society in the 1920s and then a successful scriptwriter of Hollywood films in the 1930s.

Self-educated, cultivated, and independent, Dorothy was renowned for the funny and imaginative dialogues in her stories. She was also feared because of her razor-sharp tongue. She had a weakness for animals, especially dogs and horses. She liked to adopt dogs off the street and shock her distinguished friends by taking them with her for a stroll. In one of her articles, Dorothy wrote that she would have liked to have had a horse in her apartment but that the animal was not let into the elevator by its operator.

Dorothy Parker caused a bit of a sensation when she temporarily took in two small crocodiles that someone had forgotten in a taxi. These are hardly ideal house pets! Within a year or two, they would have become at least as big as Dorothy herself, who was just under five feet tall. When the crocodiles moved into the bathtub, there was only one outcome. The cleaning lady handed in her notice.

### Dorothy Parker (1893-1967)
The daughter of a Scottish mother and a German-Jewish father, Dorothy Rothschild Parker was born in New Jersey. She wrote poetry, short stories, critiques, screenplays, and also plays for the theater. As an intimate observer of New York City life, she had her own newspaper column in which she often focused on women's rights.

# Babou

### ✦ SALVADOR DALÍ'S PAINTED CAT ✦

Images by the Spanish artist Salvador Dalí look like crazy dreams—there are melting watches, elephants with insect-like legs, and tigers jumping out of the mouths of fish. We call these pictures surreal. Salvador Dalí belonged to a group of artists called Surrealists, who created mysterious and fantastical things, beings, and spaces in their art.

When people met Salvador's pet they must have felt they were in a dream. Babou was an ocelot that Dalí gave to his private secretary, Captain Moore, as a gift in 1965. An ocelot is a small leopard from the jungles of South America. Salvador, who cultivated a long mustache like a cat's whiskers, enjoyed traveling everywhere with Babou. Once, when he brought Babou with him to a restaurant, he assured a frightened diner that Babou was just a normal pet cat that he had painted like a leopard.

Salvador sometimes traveled from France to America on a huge luxury liner with his wife, Gala. Even though luxury pet services were available onboard the ship, with carpeted corridors to walk one's pets, Salvador preferred to take Babou out for walks on the deck, much to the concern of their fellow passengers.

As much as he tried, Babou could not contain his wild nature. In the Paris hotel where he lived with Salvador, he would claw the furniture to shreds. Silk sofas are not the best environment for an ocelot! The difficulties only doubled after Captain Moore found a pal for Babou, a female ocelot named Bouba. When the Captain stopped working for Salvador, he took both ocelots with him. Salvador soon found a replacement. At the end of the 1970s he was often seen strolling around Paris with an anteater on a leash …

### Salvador Dalí (1904-1989)

Salvador Dalí was born in Figueres, Spain. He exhibited his first paintings in his home town at the age of fifteen. There is a museum there that he created to display his many different works. Salvador drew, painted, wrote, made movies, designed stage sets, and built objects. When he joined the Surrealists in the 1930s, his "riddle-like images" made him famous worldwide.

# Bibo

## ⤛ ALBERT EINSTEIN'S SAD PARROT ⤜

Albert Einstein inherited his musical talent and sense of humor from his mother, while his enthusiasm for the natural sciences came from his father. After completing his studies in mathematics, Albert took a job as a clerk, which bored him intensely. You might say this was a stroke of genius, as the job gave him plenty of time to think about the laws of the universe. His discoveries made him famous around the world. And in 1921 he received a Nobel Prize for Physics.

In 1932, Albert, who was Jewish, left Germany just before Hitler came to power and moved to the United States, where he was treated as a celebrity. But Albert wasn't particularly fond of all the attention. He wanted to be left alone like his dog, Chico, and his cat, Tiger. In fact, Albert thought Chico was pretty smart for always trying to bite the mailman, who was constantly delivering bags of fan mail.

On Albert's seventy-fifth birthday, among the many gifts and cards he received was a most unexpected surprise. Someone had mailed him a parrot! But Albert quickly realized that Bibo, as he had named him, seemed depressed. (No small wonder considering the traumatic experience the bird had been ex-

posed to!) With a lot of care and patience, Albert fed Bibo by hand to help him recover. But what really revived Bibo's spirits were the jokes Albert liked to tell. Although Bibo didn't understand a word, it did not matter because it was the attention of his new friend and the bursts of laughter that got him back on his feet again. Once again Albert had shown a genius for solving problems.

### Albert Einstein (1879-1955)
Albert Einstein was born in Germany. He spent much of his youth in Munich, studied in Switzerland, and later taught in Berlin. After the Nazi rise in 1933, he continued his career as a scientist in Princeton, New Jersey, where he lived, taught, and carried out research until his death in 1955. Thanks to Albert's powers of observation, curiosity, and intelligence, today we are able to understand the structure of the universe and the enormous energy hidden within the atom.

# Jofi

Sigmund Freud was an Austrian doctor who believed that events in childhood influenced the behaviors of adults. He developed a way to treat mental illness called psychoanalysis, in which patients and psychoanalysts searched for a cure by talking to each other.

When Sigmund was over seventy years old, he confirmed what many people had already known—dogs have a positive effect on the well-being of humans. Sigmund's own dog was named Jofi, which in Hebrew means "beauty." Jofi was a chow chow with a pretty red coat. He would become so jealous of Lün-Yu, Sigmund's other chow chow, that Sigmund was forced to return Lün-Yu to the breeder. After 1930, Jofi was the sole ruler in the Freud household, as well as his helper in the treatment room.

Sigmund had observed that Jofi recognized human feelings through her sense of smell. Whenever she felt tension, she crept snarling under the desk. If a patient was calm, she sat close by. It was important for Sigmund that his patients were relaxed during his therapy, allowing them to speak frankly and honestly about their thoughts and feelings. This is why he asked them to make themselves comfortable on a sofa. But he also found that Jofi's steady breathing as she lay curled up nearby helped to relax them. Jofi's sense of timing was also impeccable, as she would stand up and yawn when a session was over, before even Sigmund noticed the time was up. Their "collaboration" lasted seven years. When Jofi died after an operation, Sigmund was deeply saddened. "Dogs are like humans," he said, "but better."

### Sigmund Freud (1856-1939)
Sigmund Freud was born in what is now Czechoslovakia. Later, his family moved to Vienna, where Sigmund studied medicine and worked as a doctor of neurophysiology (medicine of the nervous system). His many theories about mental health and human behavior impacted not only the field of medicine, but also philosophy, literature, music, and painting.

# Diamond

## ✦ ISAAC NEWTON'S CLUMSY CHUM ✦

The English mathematician Isaac Newton spent a lot of time on his own as a child and rarely spoke with any of the other kids at school. But his mind bubbled with ideas and he constantly tinkered with inventions. After his school years, he wanted to look after his father's land, but he soon realized that he wasn't cut out for that kind of work. Instead, he went to Trinity College in Cambridge, England, where he would go on to develop important theories in the fields of mathematics, mechanics, and optical science. He left the university in 1665 to escape the Great Plague and returned to the countryside where he had plenty of time to think. Among other things, Isaac discovered the theory of gravity when he was sitting under a tree and an apple dropped onto his head.

One of the few stories known about Isaac's private life involved his dog, Diamond, who entered his life when Isaac was quite old. One day, as Isaac sat at his desk working, the doorbell rang. Diamond immediately began to bark and run around the desk anxiously, eventually leaping onto the desk and knocking candles over onto Isaac's papers. Within a matter of seconds, years of research went up in flames. Luckily, Isaac had mellowed with age. He simply clasped his hands behind his head and said, "Diamond! You have no idea what you have caused yet again!" Isaac did not have the heart to discipline his pet, even if he had caused such damage. It was an accident, after all!

### Isaac Newton (1643-1727)

Isaac Newton was born in the English county of Lincolnshire. As a mathematician, physicist, and astronomer, he made so many scientific discoveries that he became one of the most important natural scientists of all time.
For example, he discovered gravity as an energy force that holds our solar system together.
He explained natural laws in mechanics, the different colors in light, and developed many new approaches in a branch of mathematics called algebra.

# Lump

Pablo Picasso first learned to paint from his father, who was also a painter and art teacher. When he was only thirteen, he entered the Barcelona School of Fine Arts, and then went to Paris at the age of eighteen. Paris was where all artists went in the beginning of the twentieth century. They all wanted to come up with something new. Pablo, together with the French artist, George Braque, invented a whole new style called Cubism, which would change art forever. Throughout his life, Picasso never stopped trying out new styles.

Pablo always had a dog at his side. Over a dozen canine friends accompanied him throughout his life. In 1957, Pablo lived in a pretty villa on the French coast. He was already a famous artist by then. A visiting photographer had brought along his dachshund, Lump. When they arrived, Lump jumped out of the car, sniffed about in the garden and then fearlessly walked over to Picasso's boxer, Jan. The cheeky little dachshund then climbed onto Pablo's lap and began to furiously lick his face. The artist was smitten!

Lump stayed with Pablo while the photographer traveled on to his next assignment. The dachshund found himself in the lap of luxury. He was allowed to roam everywhere, including Pablo's bed and even his studio. Pablo immortalized his beloved Lump in an important series of paintings called *Las Meninas* (1957). To sharpen Lump's hunter instinct, Pablo created the shape of a rabbit using a thin layer of sugar that had been left over in a can. When he held the can up to Lump's nose, he licked the sweet bunny rabbit enthusiastically.

### Pablo Picasso (1881-1973)

Pablo Ruiz Picasso was born in Málaga, Spain, and died near Cannes in France. His extensive body of work included paintings, drawings, graphics, collages, and sculptures. The total number of his pieces is estimated to be fifty thousand. Perhaps his most well-known work is *Guernica* (1937). Picasso created this large-format, anti-war painting for the Spanish pavilion at the Paris World's Fair.

# Starling

➤ WOLFGANG AMADEUS MOZART'S FEATHERED IMITATOR ➤

Wolfgang Amadeus Mozart was a true child prodigy. Even at the age of seven, the highly talented composer and musician was on tour with his sister, Anna. His father, who wanted to make the extraordinary skills of both his children well known, organized a concert tour for the whole family to the most important cities in Europe. It was not until Wolfgang was twenty-five that he settled down as an independent composer in Vienna.

In 1784, Wolfgang walked past a pet shop near his home and heard a bird sing a familiar tune. He found out which bird had been singing—a starling—and bought it. At home he wrote down the notes of the birdsong with the comment: "That was wonderful!" To his astonishment, the melody was similar to one of his own compositions. We'll never know who invented the song first, but starlings are renowned for perfectly imitating the songs of other birds. It's possible that someone had whistled Wolfgang's song while walking past the pet store, maybe even Wolfgang himself!

Wolfgang loved his pet starling very much. So much so that after its death, he invited his friends and family to a solemn funeral in his garden. In the three years that the starling was with him, Wolfgang created some of his most important works, notably the operas *The Marriage of Figaro* (1786) and *Don Giovanni* (1787).

**Wolfgang Amadeus Mozart (1756-1791)**
Born in Salzburg, Austria, Wolfgang Amadeus Mozart wrote over six hundred compositions, even though he passed away at the age of just thirty-five. By the age of twelve, Wolfgang had already composed three operas. His final opera, *The Magic Flute* (1791), featured a character named Papageno, who attracted birds with his flute. This modest figure with a good heart had only one wish—to find a partner for life.
**Just like a starling does!**

FOR SALE

# Snowball

## ⤙ ERNEST HEMINGWAY'S LUCKY CAT ⤛

When Ernest Hemingway decided he wanted to become a writer, he got himself hired as a reporter for a Kansas City newspaper. He soon made a name for himself reporting on wars all over the world—from the First World War in Italy and the Spanish Civil War, to wars in the Middle East and China, as well as the Second World War.

After each of these tumultuous experiences, he liked to recover in nature. One of his favorite places was Key West, Florida, a small island he considered paradise on earth. Ernest loved to take a boat out to fish in the sea. One day a ship's captain gave him a fisherman's lucky charm—a cat with six toes. Fishermen liked to keep cats on board their vessels as mouse catchers. Cats with extra toes (called polydactyl cats) were the best mouse catchers because they could cling onboard no matter the weather.

Ernest named his six-toed lucky charm Snowball. The white cat quickly made itself at home. Before long the property teemed with Snowball's offspring, all with extra toes. Today Ernest's house is a museum that celebrates the writer's life and work. It's also home to around fifty polydactyl cats, all of whom are descended from Snowball.

When Ernest was awarded the Nobel Prize for Literature in 1954, he was unable to travel to Stockholm to accept the honor due to his poor health. So the prize was brought to him in Cuba, where he was living in the countryside at the time, along with his wife, eleven cats, nine dogs, a cow, an owl, and hundreds of books.

**Ernest Hemingway (1899-1961)**
Ernest Hemingway was born in Oak Park, Illinois. In the 1920s, he lived in Paris for a short period and met many famous artists and writers there, including Dorothy Parker (see 14). His best-known novel, *The Old Man and the Sea*, appeared in 1952 and was awarded the Pulitzer Prize the following year.

# Bustopher Jones, Mungojerrie & Rumpleteazer

### ⊱ T.S. ELIOT'S CATS ⊰

Thomas Stearns Eliot was a famous English poet with a very unique style. Not everyone found his poems easy to understand. However, he was able to reach one particular group of demanding readers—children.

Thomas used to write poems for his godchildren about a certain subject close to his heart. Cats! Among some of his velvety pawed characters were Bustopher Jones, Mungojerrie, and Rumpleteazer. The poet went out of his way to find the right names for his cats. He believed that if a cat was given the wrong name, it could not lift its tail or show off its whiskers. Thomas wrote amusing verses about cats and their unique behaviors. In 1939, he collected all of these poems into *Old Possum's Book of Practical Cats*. "Old Possum" was poet Ezra Pound's pet name for Thomas. It's only fitting that a pet name is in the title of Thomas's most popular book, still read by kids of all ages everywhere.

One of these children was the English composer and playwright Andrew Lloyd Webber, who was inspired by Thomas's stories to create the musical *Cats* in 1981. Even today you can take in a show to hear a chorus of Jellicle cats meow the words of Thomas's popular poems.

### T. S. Eliot (1888-1965)

Thomas Stearns Eliot was born in St. Louis, Missouri. He spent much of his time reading, especially poetry, maybe because his mother was a poet herself. After studying in literature and philosophy, he decided to live in the country of his ancestors, England. There he published novels, poems, and plays. He was awarded the Nobel Prize for Literature in 1948.

# Puce

## ⤙ HENRI MATISSE'S BLACK CAT ⤚

At first, Henri Matisse wanted to become a lawyer. If he had not become sick and bedridden for a while, his mother would not have given him paints and a brush. From that point on, Henri only wanted to paint for the rest of his life. And with that, he enrolled at the Paris Academy of Art.

Henri tried many different styles, but what excited him the most were colors. Though he had been taught to represent nature as accurately as possible, he created a totally different world of bright red and violet trees, blue faces, and yellow cats. At the beginning of the twentieth century, Henri and his fellow painters were called *les Fauves*, which means "wild beasts" in French. His paintings appealed to a wide audience, partly because of the tranquility they radiated. The source of this serenity might have been his home life, where he had created a mini-paradise with many plants, birds, a dog, and especially several cats.

When Henri was again bedridden due to illness in the 1940s, his cats Minouche, Coussi, and la Puce ("the flea") kept him company. Puce, a black cat with a small white spot on its chest, had marked his bed as her territory. Henri's cats sat for hours next to him as he worked in bed with scissors and paper to cut out shapes from colored papers and then arranged them into vibrant composition. In the final year before his death and when he was almost blind, the *Snail* was created, which at almost 3 meters in size is a celebration of colors!

### Henri Matisse (1869-1954)

Henri Émile Benoît Matisse was born in Le Cateau-Cambrésis in northern France on New Year's Eve. He was one of the most influential artists of the twentieth century. In his later life, poor health prevented him from painting on canvas and easel. Instead, he turned to cutouts, a technique where he cut shapes out of colored paper and then arranged them into masterpieces.

# Pluto & Elia

✦ LUCIAN FREUD'S MODELS ✦

The painter Lucian Freud, grandson of Sigmund Freud (see page 20), was born in Berlin. He moved to England with his family when he was ten to escape the persecution of Jews in Germany.

There are dog lovers in all generations of the Freud family, but Lucian shared a further peculiarity with his grandfather: both involved their pets in their work. While Sigmund's chow Jofi assisted in his therapy sittings, Lucian's whippet Pluto sat for him as a model.

Lucian painted true-to-life pictures. He tried to portray people and dogs on the canvas exactly as they were. This required a lot of patience from both the artist and his models. His sensitive portraits and nudes were created over months or sometimes years. Totally motionless, Pluto would peek out of the corner of one eye as Lucian applied one coat of paint after the other. Lucian worked hard to paint his subjects as openly and honestly as possible.

Viewers of his paintings felt both fascinated and uncomfortable by such vulnerability. But it's what gives his paintings such energy.

Pluto was part of Lucian's work for fifteen years. When she became older, her great, great-niece Eli took her place in the studio, while Pluto relaxed. Eli was Lucian's gift to his long-time assistant David Dawson. The two can be seen together in Lucian's last painting, *Portrait of the Hound* (2011).

### Lucian Freud (1922-2011)
Lucian Freud achieved international fame for his portraits and nudes. His career as the most important portrait painter of the twentieth century lasted over seventy years. In 2001, he even did a portrait of Britain's Queen Elizabeth II.

# Choupette

## ⊱ KARL LAGERFELD'S MEDIA STAR ⊰

For over sixty years, Karl Lagerfeld was one of the most influential fashion designers of the twentieth century. From a young age he was known for cutting photos out of magazines, closely examining the clothing styles of his friends, and drawing sketches for hours on end. He is best known for his designs for Chanel.

There was simply nothing ordinary about Karl. And the same can be said for Choupette, a white Burmese he was supposed to be caring for over Christmas 2011. She was just a couple of months old at that time and never let her "temporary" master out of her sight. The two had become inseparable. "I never thought I could fall in love like this," said Karl, who totally pampered Choupette. She ate with him at the same table, she had her own little plate, she wore a diamond-encrusted collar, and even had her own assistant! She appeared as a model herself and soon became a media star through photo sessions and fashion shows. She has her own Twitter, Facebook, and Instagram accounts, and even a book called *Choupette: The Private Life of a High-Flying Cat*.

Karl jokingly complained that the cat would soon be more famous than he was. He even said that he would have married Choupette if a marriage between man and animal were at all possible.

### Karl Lagerfeld (1933-2019)
Karl Otto Lagerfeld was born in Hamburg, Germany, but spent most of his life in Paris, France. In his career as fashion designer, designer, photographer, and costume designer, he worked for major fashion houses and brands. He designed male and female fashion under his own name continuously from 1974. From 1983, he was active as the creative director and chief designer of the French fashion house Chanel, leading it to international success.

# Stanley & Boodgie

## ⤙ DAVID HOCKNEY'S DACHSHUNDS ⤚

Although David Hockney was born in chilly, rainy England, since 1964 he has spent most of his life in sunny California. His paintings often capture the sun-drenched swimming pools, villas, and gardens of the rich and beautiful. He often swapped his brushes and pencils for cameras, fax machines, and even his iPad.

When he first encountered his neighbor's dachshunds in the Hollywood Hills overlooking Los Angeles in the 1980s, he immediately fell in love. From then on, David, Stanley, and Boodgie were always together. David has captured his dachshunds on canvas countless times. He set up easels all over the house to be able to paint the animals in all sorts of poses, whether sleeping, lying, sitting, curled up, paws raised in the air, blinking with one eye, or cuddled up on their dog cushions. Sometimes just one alone and sometimes both together. *Dog Days*, an entire book containing eighty-four of these images, was published in 1998.

As David explains, "These two lovely, little creatures are my friends. They are intelligent, loving, funny and often bored. They watch me at work and I observe the warm shapes that they make together, their sadness and their joys." And Hollywood dogs seem to somehow know that a picture of them is being made. "The two of them, and this is typical of Hollywood dogs, pose with the bored expression of someone who is used to being considered very special." And indeed, Stanley and Boodgie are very special to David!

### David Hockney (*1937)

David Hockney was born in Bradford, England. After studying at the Royal College of Art, David embarked on a brilliant career as an artist, graphic designer, photographer, lecturer, and stage designer. He became world famous in the 1960s for his cool, brightly painted images of California. David constantly bowled people over with his use of different techniques, ranging from classic painting styles to photo collages, which he made using his iPhone and iPad.

# Bo & Chia

## ⤙ GEORGIA O'KEEFFE'S CHOW CHOWS ⤚

Georgia O'Keeffe was a true pioneer who led an independent life and did not allow herself to be controlled in her artistic work. In her time, it was unusual for a woman to become a painter. Even as a child on her family farm in Wisconsin in the early 1900s, Georgia felt a strong bond with art and nature. Later, she would find a place where they could be both wonderfully brought together.

While in New York City during the 1930s, where Georgia painted its bold new skyscrapers, she decided to visit the New Mexico desert. She was fascinated by the light, by the colors of the soil, the stones, and the animal bones she found there. In 1940, she settled down in a simple mud brick house in the New Mexico village of Abiquiú.

Shortly after she moved in, a neighbor thought the painter seemed a bit lonely and gave her two jet-black chow chow puppies—Bo and Chia. Georgia instantly fell in love. Whenever she went to paint in the desert or to the Cerro Pedernal mesa, which can be seen in many of her paintings, Bo and Chia were by her side. Her connection to the animals was very intense. Even as her friends died, she felt her best companions—Bo and Chia—were still with her. She talked about them in her letters to friends and family and was devoted to the needs of the "little people," as she called her chows. In 1972, she even became a member of the local Chow Chow Club.

**Georgia O'Keeffe (1887-1986)**
**Georgia O'Keeffe was born in Sun Prairie, Wisconsin. She went to Chicago to study art and then to New York. It was there that she met the photographer, Alfred Stieglitz, whom she married in 1924. He took over three hundred photographs of her. Some of these can be seen in the Georgia O'Keeffe Museum in Santa Fe, New Mexico. Her best-known paintings are close-ups of flowers in bold colors. She received many prizes in her lifetime, including the Presidential Medal of Freedom, which is the highest award an individual can receive in the United States.**

# Bimbo

## ⤙ PAUL KLEE'S WHITE TOMCAT ⤙

Paul Klee created art with both hands. With his left he painted and drew the bow of his violin, with the right he wrote and held the violin. His grandmother gave him his first set of crayons. Paul would go on to become an outstanding violinist and a world-famous painter.

Paul had cats at his side throughout his life: Mietz, Nuggeli, Chuzli, Bäreli, Joggeli, Seppi, Köbi, Bübli, Chrütli, and Nutz were some of his feline friends. In 1906, a tabby named Fritzi joined his family. When he was away, he asked after Fritzi in every letter he wrote to his wife, asking her to pass on "paw tap" or "cold wet nose kiss" greetings.

Later, when Paul was a professor at the Bauhaus art school in Weimar, Germany, a white angora cat named Bimbo sat in his studio as his constant companion. She would watch from the window sill as the artist mixed his paints for such famous pictures as *The Mountain of the Sacred Cat* (1923) and the *Cat and Bird* (1928).

Paul immortalized his favorite animals in over fifty artworks and 250 mostly blurry photographs. Ernst Ludwig Kirchner, a painter friend of Paul Klee, knew about the special relationship between Paul and Bimbo. In his own piece, *Hommage à Klee* (1935/36), the painter is holding a violin in his hand while Bimbo sits near his shoulder.

### Paul Klee (1879-1940)

Paul Klee was born near Bern, Switzerland. He moved to Munich in 1906 and later became a German citizen. He was a professor at the influential Bauhaus art school between 1920 and 1931. Given the versatility of his work, he is one of the most original artists of the twentieth century. Today, his work is honored at the Zentrum Paul Klee in Bern.

© for the Spanish edition: Zahorí Books, 2019
Title of the original edition: Amistades Animales
© for the English edition: 2020,
Prestel Verlag, Munich · London · New York
A member of Verlagsgruppe Random House GmbH
Neumarkter Strasse 28 · 81673 Munich
© for the illustrations: Katherine Quinn, 2019
© for the texts: Ana Gallo, 2019

Prestel Publishing Ltd.
14-17 Wells Street
London W1T 3PD

Prestel Publishing
900 Broadway, Suite 603
New York, NY 10003

Library of Congress Control Number: 2019950499
A CIP catalogue record for this book is available from the British Library.

Translation: Paul Kelly
Project management: Melanie Schöni
Copyediting: John Son
Production management: Susanne Hermann
Typesetting: ew print & medien service GmbH
Printing and binding: OZGraf

Verlagsgruppe Random House FSC® N001967

Printed in Poland

ISBN 978-3-7913-7425-3
www.prestel.com